The Great Celestial Cow

'Sita, the heroine, leaves her treasured cow, Princess, in her native Indian village and sets out with her two children to join her husband in Leicester . . . Ms Townsend is a writer with a fresh and original vision.'
Michael Billington, *Guardian*

'This tender, funny, feminist play is on one level about the tribulations of Asians in England, it is also about how hideously men still treat women.'
Giles Gordon, *Spectator*

'A lovely play, crammed with well-observed, deeply felt detail that hits hard.'
Anthony Masters, *The Times*

Sue Townsend lives in Leicester. Her plays include **Womberang** (Soho Poly, London, 1979); **Dayroom** (Croydon Warehouse Theatre, 1981); **The Ghost of Daniel Lambert** (Leicester Phoenix, 1981); **Bazaar and Rummage** (Royal Court Theatre Upstairs, 1982, BBC Television, 1983); **Groping for Words** (Croydon Warehouse, 1983); **The Great Celestial Cow** (The Joint Stock Company, 1984); **The Secret Diary of Adrian Mole aged 13¾ – The Play** (Leicester Phoenix, 1984), and **Ten Tiny Fingers, Nine Tiny Toes** (Library Theatre, Manchester, 1989). Her other published work includes **The Secret Diary of Adrian Mole Aged 13¾** (1982); **The Secret Diary of Adrian Mole Songbook** (in collaboration with Ken Howard and Alan Blaikley, 1985); **The Growing Pains of Adrian Mole** (1984) and **The True Confessions of Adrian Albert Mole** (1989). Her novel **Rebuilding Coventry** was published in 1988.

Sue Townsend

The Great
Celestial Cow

Methuen Drama

A Methuen Drama **Modern Play**

First published in 1984 as a Methuen Drama Paperback in association with the Royal Court Theatre, Sloane Square, London SW1. Revised and re-issued in the Methuen Modern Plays series in 1990 by Methuen Drama

A CIP catalogue record for this book is available from The British Library.

ISBN 0-413-64630-0

The photograph on the front cover is by John Haynes.
The photograph of Sue Townsend on the back cover is by Tessa Musgrave.

Introduction

I started to write **The Great Celestial Cow** after seeing four Asian women laughing in a street in Leicester. They were leaving a factory and were obviously happy to be out in the fresh air for a while until their household duties claimed them.

When I say that I started to 'write' the play, I don't mean that I rushed home grabbed a pen and wrote there and then. What I mean is that I started to think about the lives of Asian women in Leicester.

Many of these women come from rural backgrounds. It is common for their husbands to come to Leicester, find a job, establish a hon.c and then send for their wives and children. Consequently, during their husbands' absence, the women enjoy a certain autonomy. I thought how difficult it must be to transplant yourself to a cold urban environment with a different set of rules and customs where the language is foreign and where suddenly your status is reduced.

I put myself in their place and knew that, were our positions to be reversed, I would go quietly mad.

The play was commissioned by the Joint Stock Theatre Company and performed after a period of research, a ten week writing gap and four weeks' rehearsal during which the actors and director Carole Hayman contributed to the final performance script. It is their play as well as mine.

The Great Celestial Cow was the cause of much heated debate amongst the (mostly male) Asian community in Leicester. There was resentment because I was a white woman writer. How dare I criticise the Asian family. Yet I watched many of our critics laughing (and sometimes obviously moved) as they watched the play, only to raise their voices in anger during the discussions after the show.

I noticed my first grey hairs during the research period. More appeared in the ten weeks of writing and by the time the play had finished its tour and was at the Royal Court I was reaching for the hair dye. Yet **The Great Celestial Cow** remains my favourite play. It was difficult to write and is difficult to stage but it can be quite magical when it works.

Sue Townsend
Leicester
July 1990

The Great Celestial Cow was first presented by Joint Stock Theatre Group at the Leicester Haymarket Studio on 15 February 1984, and on tour, before opening at the Royal Court Theatre, London, on 30 March 1984, with the following cast:

Spirit of Kali **2nd Official** **Mother-in-law (Dadima)** **Muslim Girl**	Zohra Segal
Prem **Old Age Pensioner** **Rose** **Cow in Field** **Auctioneer**	Lou Wakefield
Princess **Rachel** **Lila** **Classical Indian Dancer** **Indira** **Ram** **Nurse**	Shreela Ghosh
Princess **Martin** **Harmonium Player** **Kishwar** **Asian Elder** **Mr Patel** **Cow in Field**	Bhasker
Sita	Souad Faress
Daheba **Stewardess** **1st Official** **Fat Auntie (Masi)** **Liberal** **Sarla**	Jamila Massey
Bibi **Stallholder** **Cow in Nativity** **Anita** **Dr Mistry**	Feroza Syal
Naal Player **Photographer** **New Owner** **Raj** **2nd Fat Auntie** **Harold**	Dev Sagoo

Directed by Carole Hayman
Designed by Amanda Fisk
Lighting Designer Geoff Mersereau
Choreographer Sue Lefton
Costumes by Pam Tait/Amanda Fisk
Musical Director Lizzie Kean

Note on the layout

A speech usually follows the one immediately before it but:

1) when one character starts speaking before the other has finished, the point of interruption is marked /

eg. **Mother-in-law** Sita's chappatis are too hard/for my teeth.
    Bibi   I like them.

2) a character sometimes continues speaking right through another's speech

eg. **Bibi**   All that petting and baby/talk? It would drive me
    Mother-in-law Raj is too soft with her.
    Bibi   mad. Bugger off until the floor is dry.

3) sometimes a speech follows on from a speech earlier than the one immediately before it, and continuity is marked * or **

eg. **Bibi**   All that petting and baby/talk? It would drive me
    Mother-in-law Raj is too soft with her.
    Bibi   mad. Bugger off until the floor is dry.**
    Fat Auntie   She wants to be head of the house, you know.*
    Prem   **No, I want to walk on it.
    Bibi   You dare.
    Mother-in-law *What would happen to us if she was?

where 'the floor is dry' is the cue to 'No, I want to walk', and 'head of the house, you know' is the cue to 'What would happen to us'.

Act One

1975

Early morning in a village in India.
*A **Little Boy** dressed in white shorts and vest is dragging a pile of grass towards a rickety compound. Inside the compound a **Cow** raises its head. It makes an aggressive warning noise. The **Little Boy** backs off slightly.*

Prem Today is the last day you send my heart diving.

*He unties the bundle, throws grass to the **Cow**.*

Stupid cow! I don't like you. Bad luck for you eh? But you started it! Go on, eat!

*The **Cow** doesn't eat.*

I got up before I was awake to cut that grass. (*He shouts.*) Eat! Or choke on it! Do something! Stupid, idiot cow!

*The **Cow** repeats the warning noise. The **Boy** backs off.*

(*He shouts louder.*) I'm going to England and you're staying here! (*He laughs.*) When I am flying over the ocean and Buckingham Palace you will still be here! When I am looking at the queen and the Bay City Rollers you will be a million miles away! When I am sitting on the toilet in Leicester (*He laughs, shouting.*) you will be here standing in your own dirt!

*A **Woman** carrying a pail runs on, she is **Sita**, the **Boy**'s mother. She is angry.*

Sita Don't shout at her, you will ruin her milk! (*Stroking the **Cow**.*) There there, he is excited. He is only a little boy. His head is full of the aeroplane.

*The **Cow** eats.*

(*To **Prem**.*) Without her milk you and I and your sister would have starved, when Bapu's money didn't come.

Prem Is starve the same as hungry?

Sita No and I hope you never find out the difference for yourself.

Prem I am always hungry. In Leicester I will eat and eat and eat until my belly bursts open.

Sita *milks the* **Cow.**

Sita Yes and then I will have to stitch you up. More work for me. It is five-thirty, go and tell your sister to come. Tell her to look her best for the photograph. Tidy hair and a clean face.

Prem *dawdles off.*

Sita *sings a small snatch of a lament.*

A **Neighbour** *enters. She is carrying a bundle of clothes. She walks past* **Sita** *ignoring her.*

Sita Daheba!

Daheba *turns slowly, looks at* **Sita.**

Daheba After six months of silence you speak to me?

Sita Yes I am leaving here today.

Daheba I know, you are going to Leicester. My uncle's cousin is there.

Sita (*slightly put out*) So, you know, do you, which flight I am taking?

Daheba No but you are landing at Heathrow.

The **Women** *smile.*

Sita A silly quarrel. I can't remember what it was about.

Daheba I can, you said that my daughters would never marry.

Sita But it was meant as a compliment to you. You are a magnificent mother, who would want to leave you?

Daheba (*bows her head accepting the lie*) The cow is sold satisfactorily?

Sita Oh yes. I am satisfied with the price.

Daheba And the milking bucket?

Sita No, not the bucket.

Daheba You are perhaps taking it with you?

Sita A bucket on an aeroplane?

Daheba Ridiculous! So the bucket remains here, without an owner.

The **Women** *sigh.*

Sita Of course there is hand luggage.

Daheba True.

Sita But a bucket is heavy.

Daheba And noisy. Clank, clank, clank. It would draw attention to you. Make a bad impression. English people would say, 'Tuh! Here comes another dirty immigrant with her children and bucket.'

Sita English people would say that?

Daheba Oh yes. My uncle's cousin has been there for five years now.

Sita But I am not an immigrant. I am a British subject.

Daheba They call us all immigrants over there.

Sita Then I will tell them the truth.

Daheba You can speak English can you?

Sita No, but I will learn.

Then to the **Cow**.

Thank you, good girl.

Daheba So, the bucket.

Sita *finishes milking. She carries the bucket out of the compound.*

Sita Yes, this is a good bucket. No leaks. No rust. Comfortable to carry. Hard to leave behind.

Bibi *enters. She is eleven years old. She is dressed in her best clothes. She has ribbons in her hair.*

Bibi Do I look all right?

Sita Let me see you.

Sita *goes to* **Bibi** *and gives her a severe motherly inspection. She tightens the hair ribbons etc.*

Show me your teeth.

Bibi *bares her teeth.*

Good, good. Yes you are as pretty as you can be.

Daheba (*to* **Bibi**) How tall you are. I hope you will not continue to grow or you will be nudging the stars.

Sita She will outshine them if she does.

Daheba But so lanky for eleven!

Prem (*off*) He's here, he's here!

Prem *enters.*

Daheba Ah, here is the one to melt hearts.

Prem He's here, Ma.

A **Photographer** *enters on a bike. He is wearing a mixture of Indian and Western clothes. The* **Women** *draw their scarves over their heads.*

Photographer Your son has told me that you want the photograph taken here. Is that true?

He looks round in disgust.

Sita Yes.

Photographer It will be most difficult, the light . . .

He peers at the sky.

Sita There is not enough light or too much?

Prem *hovers around the bike.*

Daheba Shush! He is a professional you know. You have a studio don't you?

Photographer Yes. The light in my studio is perfect. It is from Germany. (*To* **Prem**.) Don't touch the spokes.

Prem The light is from Germany?

Photographer My lamps are from Germany.

Prem Is Germany near England?

Photographer Yes. Very near. That's why they are always fighting.

Prem England won both times.

He does fighting acting at his sister.

Bibi Don't.

Sita Prem! Don't! (**Prem** *stops.*)

Prem Who is to be in the photograph?

Daheba *looks eager.*

Sita My children and Princess.

Photographer (*to* **Daheba**) You are Princess?

The **Children** *and* **Sita** *laugh.*

Daheba (*angry*) You dare to call me a cow? My husband and father-in-law will come and smash up your German lamps. (*Scornfully.*) Studio! Ha! A white sheet hung on a wall and he calls it a studio. (*To* **Sita**.) Keep your old pail. I don't want it! (*She exits.*)

Photographer Are the people in this village mad? What did I say? (*Pause.*) Is her husband tall?

Bibi I don't know. He doesn't leave his bed.

Prem He's dying.

Photographer Oh good. I have decided I will photograph you all in your house. I cannot work in these conditions.

The **Children** *laugh.*

Is there some sickness in this village that makes you all laugh and get angry for nothing? If so tell me and I will go back to my bed in my own village.

Sita Princess is our cow. You cannot take her photograph in our house because she will not get through the door.

Photographer You have brought me here to take a *cow's* photograph?

Sita Yes. Our cow has been good to us. I want to take a small piece of her with me.

Bibi We are going to England.

Photographer Then cut off one of her ears and take that because I refuse to take a cow's photograph. You bring me here at this terrible hour . . . the sleep still in my eyes . . .

Sita I am going to pay you! And your trousers show that you need the money.

Photographer Let me see your money.

Sita *shows money.*

I'm not used to this third class situation. I am going to Delhi in two years' time you know.

He sets up his rickety tripod, fusses around with camera and film.

Prem Don't touch the spokes, Bibi.

Photographer A big studio on a fashionable thoroughfare.

Bibi I'm only looking, no harm.

Prem Don't waste your eyes. You won't ride a bike, but I will.

Sita (*instructing the* **Children**) Prem, don't crowd in front of Princess. She is the most important. I won't see her again. Kneel down. Put your arms around each other. Smile. (*To the* **Photographer**.) Go ahead.

Photographer What about you. Don't you want your photograph taken?

Sita No, I am there with my children. Ready, steady.

Blackout.

Flash of the photograph.

Scene Two

The aeroplane. **Bibi**, **Prem** *and* **Sita**, *sitting. Jet noise. Lights dim to half light.*

A **Stewardess** tucks blankets around the family.

Stewardess Sleep well.

Prem Ma, I can't go to sleep.

Bibi Tell him to be quiet, Mama.

Sita Prem, close your eyes now.

Prem I want to see the stars.

Bibi Shush. If you are not quiet Kali will come.

Prem Which one's Kali?

Sita The wife of Shiva.

Prem He's the best god, isn't he?

Sita Yes.

Bibi Kali was better than him. When Shiva was sleeping she killed the demons, didn't she?

Sita Yes but Shiva was thinking, not sleeping like you two will be soon. So demons came and started eating the villagers.

Bibi So the villagers that were left went to the top of the mountain and tried to wake Shiva, but he wouldn't wake so Kali . . .

Prem Let Ma tell it, Bibi.

Sita Shush. So Kali looked at the death and destruction that the demons were causing and a strange thing happened.

Bibi Oh yes I know, she changed into a monster!

Sita With many arms and many legs and a garland made of skulls and a hideous face like this.

Prem *cuddles closer to* **Sita**.

. . . but terrible though she was and even using many swords she could not defeat the demons. They fought for many days and nights.

Bibi (*sleepily*) Nine.

Sita Each time she killed one demon many more would spring up in its place formed by the drops of blood.

Bibi The worst bit now.

Sita So Kali drank their blood.

Prem Ugh!

Sita And maddened and made terrible by it, *she* started to kill the villagers.

Prem I would have killed her easy.

Sita No. She became all-powerful.

Prem Not better than Shiva?

Bibi Don't interrupt Prem.

Sita The villagers woke Shiva somehow. He came down from his mountain and tried to stop his wife. But he couldn't, and Kali fought him down to the ground and was about to kill him with a big sword when Shiva said 'No don't, I'm your husband'. And Kali looked down at him from her great height and she said 'Husband, I will not take your life'.

Prem So it ended happily?

He snuggles down.

Sita I don't know. I suppose it does.

Bibi For the villagers.

Pause.

Prem I bet he beat her when he got her home.

Sita Yes. Now sleep, and when you wake up you will be in England.

The **Children** *get into sleeping attitudes.* **Sita** *stares straight ahead.*

Princess appears.

Goodbye Princess.

Princess's **New Owner** *appears.*

New Owner C'mon cow what are you doing lying down? On your feet! C'mon, on your feet you lazy cow, there is work to be done.

He whacks **Princess**. *She makes an anguished cow noise.*

Sita *screws her eyes shut unable to bear it.*

Scene Three

The arrival lounge at Heathrow airport. The family sit on the floor, they have been waiting for two hours. **Bibi** *has the bucket on her lap.*

An announcement from the loudspeaker.

Loudspeaker Would Mr Raj Prakash come to the enquiry desk where his family are waiting for him. Mr Raj Prakash. Please come to the enquiry desk.

A uniformed **Official** *approaches.*

1st Official (*London working-class accent*) Mrs Prakash? Would you mind moving on to one of the benches please. You're in the way here. (*Pause.*) No English?

Sita Leicester. (*She shows documentation, passports.*)

1st Official Yes. Leicester. Now if you wouldn't mind moving.

2nd Official *approaches.*

2nd Official She still here?

1st Official Her old man ain't turned up has he?

2nd Official He's probably changed his mind, got halfway down the M bloody 1 and threw a wobbler.

They laugh, the **Children** *look up and smile.*

1st Official You can't blame him can you. He's had five years of freedom over here, then his missus and kids and a bloody bucket turn up.

2nd Official They'll cramp his style a bit.

1st Official Not half.

2nd Official Mind you the Asians are good family people . . . Look after each other . . . You know, the old people . . . Bit like the Jews.

1st Official Yeah, how's *your* mum?

2nd Official (*evasively*) Oh all right, (*Small pause.*) I think. We don't get over as often as we'd like . . . but it's a nice place . . . for an institution like.

1st Official Still you couldn't have had her with you, could you, Mick?

2nd Official No, her wheelchair knocked every bit of paint off the skirting boards. An' Brenda and her never did get on . . .

1st Official Well don't you feel guilty about it . . . You got your own life to live ain't you? Your mum's had hers.

2nd Official That's the problem. You see she *ain't* really. She's lived, but she ain't had what I'd call a *life*.

1st Official Well they didn't in the old days did they? They was too busy livin' to have a life.

2nd Official Well my old woman's makin' up for it, I tell you, the way she's going . . . out every bloody night. Weight Watchers, nightschool, jewellery parties . . .

1st Official 'Bout time you started cracking down.

2nd Official An' she's got opinions about everything.

1st Official Opinions?

2nd Official Yeah. Bloody this, bloody that. She'll be standin' for the bloody GLC next.

1st Official An' I'd vote for her if she'd put a few white people at the top of the housing list for a change.

2nd Official I know, dis-bloody-gustin'.

1st Official (*to the family group*) Right come on now! Quicki quicki, move to benchi!

*The **Officials** go.*

Prem What is he saying Mama?

Sita How do I know?

He is telling us to move I think. We must move, Ma. Look,
ody else is sitting on the floor.

ita Exactly, so your father will be sure to see us won't he?

Bibi What time is it, Ma?

Sita Milking time.

Bibi Morning or evening?

Sita Evening. (*She cries.*)

Two hippies, **Rachel** *and* **Martin**, *watch.*

Rachel Oh Martin look. Oh how *sad.*

Martin Yeah.

Rachel Do you think somebody's been, you know, *awful* to them?

Martin Could be.

They stand over the family group.

Rachel Ask them what's wrong. Go on, Martin you're good with
kids.

Martin Er . . . er . . . (*He pats his chest*) 'Mitra'.

Prem Tell the nasty man to go away, Ma.

Rachel (*pats her chest*) 'Mitra'. Don't cry! Me and him we've come
back from India. Bombay, Calcutta, Delhi, Madras. We love your
country. (*She smiles.*)

Martin Yeah . . . 'Mitra'.

Bibi They are saying 'friend' in Gujerati I think.

Prem Mama! Tell him to go away.

Rachel What did he say?

Martin Dunno. (*He squats down.*) Hey. C'mon kids.

Rachel If only we could explain that we *know* India and its people.
We *know* it.

Martin (*to* **Sita**) Spiritually . . .

Rachel *puts her hands together and bows to* **Sita**.

Rachel You are my sister.

Sita *nods, baffled.*

Martin C'mon Rachel. I gotta get to the bank.

Rachel Look what's more important Martin, helping this poor, ignorant family, or cashing your bloody traveller's cheques?

Martin Look, don't pull that moral superiority shit on me again, right? I've had six fucking months of it. It's my traveller's cheques that have paid for your spiritual awareness right?

Rachel I shouldn't have come back. I should have stayed. I belong there. They need my skills.

Martin Yeah, they're crying out for English Literature degrees right?

Rachel I could dig an Artesian well! I could advise on basic hygiene . . . and Swami Niranda invited me back.

Martin Yeah, and told you to bring five hundred fucking pounds.

Rachel He didn't!

Bibi What are the dirty people saying?

Martin He did!

Sita They are quarrelling.

Prem She doesn't like his smelly face.

The **Children** *laugh.*

Sita Shush. Remember your manners. Don't laugh at the misfortunes of others.

Rachel *and* **Martin** *go off, still arguing.*

Prem When's Bapu coming?

Bibi Soon, soon. Here eat this. Keep your mouth busy. (**Bibi** *gives* **Prem** *a chappati.*)

The noise of the arrival lounge; slow fade of lights.

Scene Four

The family is sleeping on a bench in the arrival lounge. **Raj Prakash** *and his elderly* **Mother** (**Dadima**) *and* **Aunt** (**Masi**) *approach.* **Raj** *looks down at his family. His* **Mother** *goes to wake the group.* **Raj** *restrains her.*

Raj No.

Mother-in-law So son, how do you feel at this moment?

Fat Auntie (*broken voiced*) His heart is full and so are his eyes. (*She takes out a handkerchief.*)

Mother-in-law No let me. (*She mops* **Raj***'s tears.*) My grandchildren! (*Pause.*) Your wife has lost her beauty son. (*She then wipes her own eyes with the handkerchief.*)

Fat Auntie Children drain beauty away, they put the lines on our foreheads and the white in our hair.

Raj I hardly know her.

Mother-in-law Tired, she is tired. A long flight, remember Masi.

Fat Auntie Ai, ai, ai. So long. My head was in the clouds for a week.

Raj But so different.

Fat Auntie In five years people change, a baby becomes a child and a young woman becomes an old woman. That's how it is.

Mother-in-law Wake them. I want to go back to Leicester. I don't like it here, I can't hear my thoughts.

A jet starts to take off. They mime their meeting.

Prem *is greeted first. Then* **Raj** *and* **Sita** *politely greet each other, but* **Prem** *comes between them.*

The plane noise stops.

Come on everybody. Pick up the luggage. (*To* **Prem**.) Not you little one. Come on Bibi. Masi, you help.

They collect the baggage and bundles, **Bibi** *picks up the bucket.*

Why are you carrying a bucket? Put it down.

Bibi It's mother's. I'm in charge of it.

Sita You remember Princess, Raj? It's her milking bucket.

Raj There are no cows in Leicester, Sita. I have written and told you many times about Leicester.

Mother-in-law No land. Only parks . . .

Fat Auntie They are owned by the council and you may not walk on the grass. In some parks you may but in others there is a sign.

Mother-in-law 'Keep off the grass.'

Raj And our house opens on to a street. And the street is bu[...] cars and buses and lorries.

Mother-in-law I already have a bucket, it is red and made of plastic.

Sita I would like to keep it, please.

Raj But how will it look? We have to pass many people before we reach the minibus. No, I refuse to be seen walking with a bucket.

Prem Ma wants to buy a cow, she told me on the plane.

Bibi You were naughty, she told you stories so that you would sit still. Bapu are you going to beat Prem?

Raj (*laughing*) No, why should I beat my beloved son? I haven't seen him for five years.

He picks up **Prem** *and hugs him.*

Bibi I wish somebody would. He pulls my hair.

Laughter.

Mother-in-law Come on, I want to go home. (*To* **Bibi**.) Pick it up child, it won't carry itself.

They exit carrying luggage and bundles. **Sita** *walks behind them. She has picked up the bucket and hidden it under a piece of cloth.*

Scene Five

Raj *and* **Sita** *alone in their room.* **Sita** *looks around,* **Raj** *sits on the bed.*

Raj So what do you think of it?

Sita Such a big room for two people. Do we sleep alone?

Raj We do tonight, come here.

Sita *approaches him.*

Raj Take off your sari, I want to look at you.

Sita And a window!

Raj Sita, let me look at you

Sita There's no hurry Raj.

Raj After five years there's no hurry? You are my wife. Take off your sari, Sita.

...dia you would wait a little. Kiss me. Use fine words to

...Who can blame me for being impatient? Come here.

...*a approaches shyly.* **Raj** *gets up and unfastens* **Sita's** *sari.*

Raj (*quietly*) I will unfasten you as I did on our wedding night, remember?

He unwinds the sari slowly.

You were so young, and very beautiful. The most beautiful girl in the village. But tired, too tired to move. I had to teach you everything, didn't I Sita? I hope I was (*Still unwinding the sari.*) patient with you. I didn't want to frighten you. You lay still in my arms for the first months but then you began to move and . . . (*Still unwinding the sari.*) . . . how much longer? Are women wearing so much cloth in India now? Help me Sita.

Sita *clutches her sari to her.*

Sita I am afraid for you to see my body.

Raj Why? Is it scarred or diseased in some way? (*He laughs.*)

Sita No, but I have not cared for it as *you* liked. There was no time. And I lost interest in how I looked and only took pride in what my body could do. There was always so much work.

Raj Your work will be easier here. There are machines for cooking and washing. Your hands and feet will soon lose their roughness.

Sita How will I fill my time?

Raj I have arranged a job for you. You start at Mr Lakhani's dress factory on Monday. It is easy work. You will like it there and earn £55 a week. I told Mr Lakhani that you are an excellent machinist.

Sita *remains still.*

Now come to bed and prove that you are also an excellent wife.

Sita Raj, I feel frozen.

Raj I will plug in the electric fire.

Sita No, I'm not cold, but I'm frozen.

Raj *takes* **Sita** *in his arms, kisses her neck. Music; Indian film dance drama.* **Raj** *does melodramatic seduction acting,* **Sita** *is impassive. Suddenly* **Raj** *grows impatient and pulls* **Sita's** *sari, twirling her round and round.* **Sita** *is revealed in her petticoat and under-blouse.*

Raj *is about to remove her blouse when* **Prem** *runs into the room in some distress.*

Prem I dreamed I was being eaten by a cow!

He clings to his father's legs.

Raj The cows in England are miles away in the country. You are quite safe, now go back to bed. Ma and Bapu want to be alone.

Prem No, I want to sleep with Ma. I always do don't I Ma?

Raj Not tonight. Now go to your own bed.

Prem No I won't! I want to sleep with Ma. (*Shouts.*) I want Ma! I want Ma!

Raj And I want Ma. She was mine before she was yours.

Prem But she's mine now. I don't want you to sleep in her bed.

Raj It is not her bed, it is mine. I bought it from the Co-op. (*To* **Sita**.) Leave the room Sita.

Sita Don't beat him, Raj.

Raj I won't. I have things to explain. Father to son.

Sita *exits.*

My son, there is no need for this panic. You will never leave your mother. You will grow up and marry and bring your wife to our house and your mother will train your wife and help to bring up your sons and daughters, just like Dadima does now.

When I am old and no longer the head of the house, then you will take my place, you will make the choices. You will decide how the money is spent. How much to give to the Temple, how much to allow the women. It is a big responsibility and your mother and your wife will depend on you for their happiness.

Prem So Ma will always be mine?

Raj Until the day she is taken from you by God.

Prem I won't let God take her!

Raj Good little man, we'll have another talk when you are older. Now go to bed. Sita! Sita!

Scene Six

Leicester market. Three weeks later. A fruit stall, a cacophony of sounds as stallholders compete in attracting attention. A **Woman** *stands behind her fruit stall. She is wearing a sheepskin coat and a fur hat. She blows on her hands, stamps her feet.*

Stallholder Guavas, melons, all your exotics! Come on ladies! Fresh in today! Lovely fruit. Take some home to your old man. Ba-na-nas. O-ran-ges, Coxes Pipp-ins.

A **White Woman** *approaches the stall. She is a middle-class liberal. She looks at the fruit critically.*

Liberal Have you any unripe bananas left?

Stallholder Dunno love, I'll have a look. Cold enough for you?

She sorts through bananas.

Liberal I don't know how you do it. You're awfully brave to stand out in all weathers.

Stallholder (*shouting*) Ba-na-nas. Jaffa Oranges, Cox-es Pippins.

An **Old White Woman** *comes to the stall.*

Old Woman Can I have a few of each? Only I've got me husband in the infirmary. He likes a bit of fruit but it gus off so quick, don't it. In the 'eat of an 'ospital?

Stallholder You could grow tomatoes in them wards couldn't you?

Liberal Yes, the heat actually makes one feel worse.

Stallholder I was in last year, I didn't wear me bedjacket once.

Sita *enters and hovers around the stall.*

Old Woman He's a bit fussy, couldn't I pick me own?

Stallholder Sorry duck. No handling the fruit, that's the rule. I'll pick some out for you though. Just give me a minute to serve this lady.

Old Woman Sorry. I didn't mean to butt in.

Liberal Oh, that's all right.

Sita *gesticulates towards the fruit after catching the* **Stallholder**'s *eye.*

Stallholder (*to the* **White Women**) Here we go. Pantomime time! (*Slowly and loudly.*) This twenty pence a pound. (*Pointing.*) This ten pence each. These eighteen pence. Understand? No, of course you don't bloody understand. I don't know, they come over here, push to the front of the queue . . .

Old Woman The hospital's full of black faces.

Liberal Yes. I owe my life to a black midwife.

Old Woman No, these are in the beds. Stopping us white people from having our operations.

Stallholder They're taking over. No doubt about that. There's one born every thirty seconds.

Old Woman (*alarmed*) In Leicester?

Stallholder No, the world!

Old Woman (*dismissively*) Oh that.

The **Stallholder** *is about to weigh the bananas, when she sees* **Sita** *picking up the fruit.*

Stallholder Eh! Get your dirty black hands off my fruit! People have got to eat that! They won't want it if they see you mauling it about will they?

Sita *holds an apple, uncomprehending but frightened by the violent tone.*

I said put it down! Down! This is Leicester, not Calcutta.

Liberal She doesn't understand.

The **Stallholder** *grabs the apple from* **Sita**.

Stallholder She understands all right. They want to stick to their own shops in their own districts. Not come into town stinking the bleddy place out. (*To* **Sita**.) Go away. Go on. Go away. (*To* **Liberal**.) That's thirty-nine pence, all right for you?

Liberal No. I don't want them now. I don't think you should have spoken to her like that. It was very unkind.

Stallholder It's the only way they understand.

Liberal I shan't come to this stall again.

Stallholder Well I shan't cut me wrists over that.

Liberal (*to* **Sita**) I'm awfully sorry. Look would you like a coffee? No of course not, well nice to meet you.

She holds out her hand. **Sita** *looks at it. The* **Liberal** *picks up* **Sita**'s *right hand and manufactures a handshake.*

're not all like that. At least not in Clarendon Park.

he rushes off in confusion.

Sita (*to the* **Stallholder**) Sabhat karna sikho.

Sita *exits.*

Old Woman What's she say?

Stallholder Paki talk. (*Calling after* **Sita**.) Come back when you've learnt to talk proper, like what I do! (*To the* **Old Woman**.) See how they go on?

Old Woman It's no wonder these racialists and such don't like them is it? I'm not one myself.

Stallholder Nor me. But I can feel myself turning.

Scene Seven

1976

Leicester. Outside a junior school gate. **Kishwar**, *a Muslim woman, is waiting outside the gate. She has a box of Pampers disposable nappies under her arm. She is in full Purdah, her face is completely veiled. From the school comes the sound of junior school children singing 'Away in a Manger'.* **Sita** *joins her.*

Sita They *are* late coming out today. It's twenty-five to.

Kishwar They are practising for the Christmas concert.

Sita Oh yes, I'm going to see it, are you?

Kishwar No, I am too busy tomorrow. I would like to see it . . . My daughter is an angel . . . She talks of nothing but her silver paper wings . . . (*Small pause.*) But there is singing and dancing and as you know it is forbidden for me.

Sita The singing and dancing of children?

Kishwar Yes. My husband has become very devout since we moved to this country. I did not always have this cloth between me and the world.

The sound of large numbers of children set free from school. **Prem** *and a little* **Girl** *in Muslim headdress run out of school.*

Zhora (*showing a painting*) Look Umy I painted an angel.

Kishwar Oh yes, it's very nice. But what are those lumps sticking out of its back?

Zhora That's her wings.

Prem The concert's dead good, Ma. I'm a horse.

Zhora No, you're a donkey, Mrs Mortlake said.

Prem I'm a horse. Donkeys are stupid.

Zhora Well so are you. You're only on Red Book One. Stupid git.

Kishwar Now Zhora don't be cruel. Prem has only been in England one year.

Sita He'll soon catch up. Won't you Prem?

Prem I *am* a horse. You'll see tomorrow.

Kishwar *and* **Zhora** *start to go.*

Zhora Are you coming to see me in the concert Umy?

Kishwar I'll ask.

Prem Her wings are stupid. They keep falling off. Mrs Mortlake tries to mend them but they just fall off again. Mrs Mortlake is a stupid cow!

Sita *slaps* **Prem**. *He bawls, open mouthed.* **Sita** *drags him away.*

Sita No Smarties on the way home!

Scene Eight

The school concert.

Sita *and* **Kishwar** *sit on hard chairs watching the concert. A piano plays* 'We Three Kings of Orient Are'. **Rose** *enters.*

Rose Eh up, Sita, is that anyone's seat or are you saving it? Trust me to be late. Me bleddy washer overflowed. Look there's my Delroy. (*She waves.*) Oh he's dropped his Frankincense. (*She looks anxious.*) Pick it up Delroy!

Sita Your daughter is a beautiful angel.

Kishwar Thank you. Your son looks very handsome as a donkey.

Rose Can she see?

Sita Tum dekh sakti ho.

Kishwar Han usko kaho main dekh sakti hoon.

Sita Yes she can, she's used to it now.

Rose (*to* **Sita**) Can she take it off at home?

Sita Yes, unless strangers arrive.

Rose It'd drive me mad. I can't stand anything around my face. Who makes her wear it?

Sita Kaun pehenata hai.

Kishwar Koi nahin, hamare dharm men hai.

Sita She says she wears it because it's traditional in her culture.

Rose That can't be right. I mean you wouldn't wear it out of choice would you? Shame really, she's ever so nice underneath it. I knew her before she took the veil. She's got lovely eyes. (*To* **Kishwar**.) OK?

Kishwar OK.

Rose Bloody hell, he's tripped over his dressing-gown now. He's a clumsy little sod! (*She mimes pulling a dressing-gown up, to her son.*) Sorry for swearing.

The piano changes to 'Silent Night'.

Sita I don't mind.

Rose You're not allowed to swear are you? Don't you get your hands chopped off or something?

Sita Shush Rose!

Rose Whoops a daisy, there goes Jesus, fell out of the crib! It's the same every bloody year.

Sita Who is that boy wearing the beard?

Rose That's Joseph.

Sita Who is he?

Rose He's the bloke Mary's married to.

Sita He's the father of Jesus.

Rose Well . . . No . . . Jesus is a miracle. He's God's child.

Sita Does Joseph know this?

Rose Oh he *knows*. Mary told him. But to my mind the true m.
was that Joseph believed her. I should have told my ex-husband
that Delroy was God's child instead of Winston Johnson's.

Kishwar (*to* **Sita**) Oh her wings have fallen off!

Rose (*to* **Sita**) Tell her not to worry, it is traditional in our culture.

A primary school cow enters on its way to the stage. It stands beside **Rose.**

Rose Christ what's that?

Sita (*excited*) It's a cow, oh and so pretty. Look Kishwar, I've got a
cow. Her name is Princess.

The cow goes on to the stage.

Rose That cow's name is Tracy Wainwright. I'd know them feet
anywhere.

Sita (*clapping*) Good cow. Very good.

Rose Eh shut up. You'll get us chucked out. You don't clap at a
nativity play, it's holy.

Kishwar Holy?

Sita Like Delroy's socks.

Rose You cheeky bugger, Sita. Oh don't they show you up!

Scene Nine

December 1977

Four **Women** *leaving a factory. Their scarves have slipped down. They are
laughing.*

Lila . . . And his big fat behind! . . . Waddle, waddle . . . like my
auntie-in-law dancing at my wedding!

She does a waddling impression.

It is ten years since Lakhani saw his toes!

The **Women** *laugh.*

Sarla Lila you are wicked! If Mr Lakhani heard you . . .

Anita You would get the sack.

Lila I can say what I like when I get out of his factory. He may
have bought my time, but my tongue is still my own.

Do his voice again, Lila.

Do the bit about the talking.

la takes on Mr Lakhani's physical characteristics: fat, pompous.

Lila (*Mr Lakhani's voice*) You women are talking too much. It is slowing down your work. Do you want to bankrupt me? Do you want me to have to sell my £60,000 house and my mercedes . . . and my volkswagen bus . . .

Anita He didn't say that! (*She laughs.*)

Lila (*Mr Lakhani's voice*) Do you want to take the gold from my wife's throat? Or send my children to state schools? I will sack every damned one of you unless you reach the quota.

Sarla He did say that, about the quota.

Anita He is a foolish man, nobody can reach the quota.

Sita Not even if he put sticky tape over our mouths.

Lila The next time he shouts and raves I will prick his belly with a pin and he will fly around the workshop like a balloon.

She does a balloon deflating action complete with the noise. The **Women** *shriek with laughter and clutch each other. An elderly* **Indian Man** *walks by. He looks at them disapprovingly.*

Lila (*rattling car keys*) C'mon girls. Time to go, that's it for today. Chappatis to make.

Sita Children to fetch from school.

Anita Grandfather to wash.

Sarla Mother-in-law to quarrel with.

Lila Cheer up, work tomorrow! The quota!

Women The quota!

The **Women** *go, laughing.*

Scene Ten

The Prakash living-room, the next evening.

Raj It has come to my ears that you were behaving in a shameful manner yesterday.

Sita Me?

Raj After work, laughing and shrieking in the street with low-caste women.

Sita Can't I laugh now?

Raj Not if your laughter is loud enough to cause talk in the community.

Sita Who is this outraged person you listen to?

Raj The father of my work colleague Dev. He told his wife and his wife told my mother and naturally enough she told me. This is a small community, you must be careful. I don't want to stop you working in the factory . . .

Sita Raj you wouldn't.

Raj . . . but if I hear any more bad reports on you I will have to consider it. Perhaps arrange for you to work at home.

Sita I laughed at Lila, she's so *funny*. You would have laughed if you had been there.

Raj But it doesn't matter if *I* laugh in the street.

Sita Is that fair?

Raj It's how things are.

Sita Not in India in our village.

Raj Laughter is different in a village. Here there are walls and echoes to make a woman's laughter sound defiant and coarse, and I don't want you to associate with Lila. She is a divorced woman.

Sita (*shouting*) Her husband is a lunatic who tried to set fire to her. What was she to do? Continue living with him until she was a pile of ashes?

Raj I can see that you care enough for this Lila to raise your voice in anger against me, so I forbid you to speak to her outside your workplace.

Sita Lila is my friend. She helps me with my English.

Raj There is no need for you to speak English. Anyone you need to speak to speaks your own language.

Spot on an **Asian Elder**, *who gives a speech.*

An **Indian Dancer** *performs a graceful, contained dance.*

Asian Elder As I was walking to the temple to perform my duties I saw some of our women laughing in the street. I heard the words they used to each other. They were bad words, invisible rough weapons of disrespect to the parents that gave them birth and culture.

We elders must protect our women from the invasion of Western attitudes and habits. They must be watched and guarded and cherished. They must not be allowed the terrible freedom that has ruined the family life of Westerners. Already there have been incidents, young girls complaining of restrictions, some even phoning the police and accusing their families of cruelty. One girl from our community left her home and sold her body to strangers. When I heard of this I was so ashamed I wept. Our women must not allow their bodies to be used by any man except their husbands. Sex must not be brought downstairs.

Sometimes I wonder if we were right to come here. Is it worth losing our culture just so that we play with Western toys?

When I see the bold brazen behaviour of some of our girls I wish that I was dead. For it is better to drown in a flood or starve during a famine than to see centuries of tradition wear away.

Each grain of sand once belonged to a rock. I am saving with the Bank of India, when I have enough money I will take my family home.

Scene Eleven

1977.

The Prakash living-room.

Bibi *is washing the floor on hands and knees.* **Mother-in-law** *and* **Fat Auntie** *are making chappatis.*

Mother-in-law Sita's chappatis are too hard/for my teeth.*

Bibi I like them.

Fat Auntie *She uses too much flour. I've told her but she won't listen.

Mother-in-law Raj likes soft chappatis.

Prem *enters. He looks down at* **Bibi. Mother-in-law** *and* **Fat Auntie** *smile at him.*

Bibi Wait a minute. /It's not dry yet.*

Fat Auntie We shouldn't be doing the kitchen work.

Prem *What am I supposed to do? I can't float.

Bibi Really? I thought you were a god/

Mother-in-law How many times has she burnt the lentils?

Bibi since you came to Leicester.*

Fat Auntie Twice this month.

Prem *You're jealous 'cos they like me best.

Prem *looks at* **Mother-in-law** *and* **Fat Auntie.**

Bibi All that petting and baby/talk? It

Mother-in-law Raj is too soft with her.

Bibi would drive me mad. Bugger off until the floor is dry.**

Fat Auntie She wants to be head of the house you know.*

Prem **No, I want to walk on it.

Bibi You dare.

Mother-in-law *What would happen to us if she was?

Fat Auntie She would turn me out.

Prem *walks over the floor.*

Mother-in-law I wouldn't let/her.*

Bibi /You rotten little sod!

She swipes **Prem** *with the floorcloth.*

Fat Auntie *But she might turn *you* out!

Mother-in-law Put me into an old/

Prem Cow!

Mother-in-law people's home you mean? Hai hai hai.

Bibi Do you want some more?

Prem *falls to the floor and works up to a tantrum.*

Fat Auntie
Mother-in-law } (*together*) Prem! What's wrong with/the baby?

Bibi He walked on the floor!

Mother-in-law *and* **Fat Auntie** *cuddle* **Prem.**

Fat Auntie ⎱ (*together*) Such a little one. What else is he to
Mother-in-law ⎰ do?

Bibi ⎱ (*together*) I asked him not to.
Prem ⎰ She hit me with a dirty cloth!

Mother-in-law Go upstairs to/your

Prem There's germs on it! I'll get a disease.

Mother-in-law room.

Fat Auntie She takes after her mother.

Mother-in-law Headstrong. Do as I say.

Fat Auntie Do as she says.

Bibi (*going*) Why do I always get the blame? (*To* **Prem**.) Why
bother, they've given the Academy Awards out this year.

Mother-in-law *takes* **Prem** *and talks to him in Hindi.* **Fat Auntie** *goes
back to the chappatis.*

Sita *enters.*

Sita What's the matter with him now? I could hear him in the
street.

Prem Bibi hit me with a dirty cloth!

Fat Auntie For nothing.

Sita For nothing, Prem?

Sita *looks at him long and hard.* **Prem** *drops eye contact.*

Sita ⎱ (*together*) For nothing?
Fat Auntie ⎰ Bibi has to learn respect.

Mother-in-law She must learn to control/herself.

Sita For this spoiled boy? Why do you always take his side?

Mother-in-law I have to. You know that.

Prem (*to* **Mother-in-law**) She's always going on at me, always.

Fat Auntie Never mind, we love you.

Sita I love him, but I don't like him much, not now.

Fat Auntie You don't like England either do you?

Sita Everything is so grey.

Mother-in-law If you want colour go and see a film. We are here to work and save and go back to our village important people.

Fat Auntie Why am I doing this? It is her job.

Mother-in-law And I'm not well, but I have to look after the house. You shouldn't be out working.

Sita Maji. (*She grabs her by the shoulders.*) Promise me that the next time you are unwell you will tell me and I will do your work for you.

Mother-in-law Why this sudden affection? What do you want?

Sita I want us all to share this house peacefully. I don't want you to keep this feeling of resentment against me.

Prem Masi and Dadima don't like you Ma.

Mother-in-law ⎫ (*together*) Shush.
Fat Auntie ⎭ Hold your tongue.

Sita I know. It makes me sad.

Fat Auntie (*to* **Sita**) Here, you make the chappatis!

Mother-in-law Yes. We'll take this poor boy and dress him in his lovely clothes, eh. Who's going to the dance tonight?

Prem We've been practising the stick dance at school today. I'm dead good at it.

They go.

Fat Auntie And not so much flour!

Sita *makes chappatis.* **Bibi** *enters and kisses* **Sita.**

Sita Don't worry about Prem, Bibi. I'm sure he deserved it. (*Small pause.*) You ought to dress soon.

Bibi Ma.

Sita Yes?

Bibi A terrible thing has happened to me.

Sita (*panic*) What? Are you ill?

Bibi Yes, I am bleeding.

Sita Where?

Bibi From my legs. At the top, I have such pains. Will I die?

Sita No, you won't die. You have become a woman.

She hugs **Bibi.**

I can't call you my little girl now.

Bibi I'm not ready to be a woman. I don't want to be a woman.

Sita But it's a good thing, women are strong and brave. We are the mothers of the world.

Bibi I don't want to be a mother. I might have a girl and then everyone will be angry.

Sita Silly! Silly! Have you washed yourself?

Bibi Yes, but it keeps coming back. I don't like it. I don't want to go to school tomorrow.

Sita Don't let it interrupt your life. Start as you mean to go on. I'll show you what to use. You're lucky living here – when I started my period . . .

Mother-in-law *and* **Fat Auntie** *enter.*

Masi, Maji, Bibi has started her period.

Mother-in-law Get away from the food!

Fat Auntie Why didn't you tell her?

Fat Auntie *takes over the chappatis.*

Sita I don't agree with it.

Mother-in-law (*to* **Bibi**) When you have a period you are unclean, you must not enter the kitchen. If you happen to approach a vessel of wine it will sour.

Fat Auntie If you touch any corn it will wither. Sit you under a tree, the fruit will fall. The very bees in the hive die. Iron and steel take rust.

Sita Nonsense! Old superstition. English women don't stop cooking.

Mother-in-law English women are not clean.

Fat Auntie You cannot go to Navratri now either. You may watch, but not dance.

Bibi But I want to dance.

Mother-in-law You cannot worship our Goddess if you are unclean!

Sita Our Goddess never bled?

Mother-in-law No, that is why we women worship her.

Raj *enters carrying an open* Leicester Mercury.

Raj Is there never any peace in this house? What's wrong with you all now?

Sita Raj. Our daughter became a woman today.

Mother-in-law Go out Raj. (*She pushes him.*)

Fat Auntie Don't listen!

Sita She started her period.

Raj *starts to move to* **Bibi**.

Mother-in-law In front of a man to use such words. (*She covers her ears.*)

Fat Auntie No shame!

Fat Auntie *and* **Mother-in-law** *wail*.

Sita Your mother has told Bibi she may not dance at Navratri tonight.

Raj (to **Mother-in-law**) Why not?

Mother-in-law It's not allowed, Raj. It will dishonour our family. It will insult the Goddess. Tell Bibi she may not dance.

Sita I say she will dance. Bibi, go and put your pretty clothes on.

Bibi No I'm dirty! I'm going to have a bath.

Fat Auntie No you must not bathe.

Mother-in-law She must not bathe, tell her Raj.

Sita She *will* bathe, and then she will dance. She will show our community how beautiful she is, and she will honour the Goddess. And all the while she will be bleeding, but she will hold her head high. And she will not be made to feel unclean!

Fat Auntie But not in front of the Goddess Raj!

Raj She will *not* dance Sita.

Sita Raj!

Raj She will *not* dance.

Sita She is my daughter as well, and I say she will dance. Why must we all do as you say?

Mother-in-law Your husband has spoken. Isn't that enough? (*To

Raj.) She will kill me. Every day she is questioning. You should never have left her alone in India for so long. She has developed a will of her own, she is trying to dominate you.

Sita (*quietly*) I don't want to dominate, I want to share. I want to be up there with him, not above or below, but *with* him.

Scene Twelve

Navratri music. A big hall. A shrine containing a **Goddess** *to one side. A* **Male Dancer** *enters and dances around the stage. He is joined by members of the family.* **Raj, Mother-in-law, Fat Auntie** *and* **Prem** *dance in a circle.* **Sita** *and* **Bibi** *enter.* **Sita** *is carrying the bucket.* **Bibi** *sits on a chair and watches.* **Raj** *pulls* **Sita** *into the dance.* **Raj** *drops out of the dance and takes an offering of money to the* **Goddess**. **Prem** *follows him and examines the other offerings. They rejoin the dance.*

Mother-in-law *and* **Fat Auntie** *give offerings to the* **Goddess**, *then they rejoin the dance.* **Sita** *leaves the dance and joins* **Bibi**. *She picks up the bucket and gives it to* **Bibi**. **Bibi** *pours milk from the bucket into a dish at the* **Goddess**'*s feet. The* **Goddess** *drinks the milk, then steps down from the shrine. She joins hands with* **Sita** *and* **Bibi** *and dances with them. They dance faster and laugh.*

Act Two

Scene One

The Prakash living-room. A **Bride** *is sitting. She is veiled and still. She is surrounded by* **Women** *laughing and talking.*

Mother-in-law It won't be long before she knows what it is to be a wife eh?

Fat Auntie I hope he is gentle with her. My husband frightened me so much I didn't open my eyes for a month! Never mind my legs!

2nd Fat Auntie You couldn't believe what you were seeing eh?

Fat Auntie It was a new sight!

Mother-in-law But you got used to it eh?

Laughter.

Fat Auntie Oh yes, but it didn't last long.

She lapses into melancholy.

2nd Fat Auntie No, no, I won't let you tell us about your years as a barren widow. We have heard it a thousand times. Come on, get up and dance with me.

She pulls **Fat Auntie** *to her feet.*

Come on! Everybody dancing! Come on old women, show these young girls how to dance. They are as stiff as broom handles. Bend! Bend! Dip and bend.

The **Women** *dance in a circle, young and old. The* **Bride** *sits with downcast eyes.*

At the end of the dance **Prem** *is led in.*

2nd Fat Auntie I hope you are prepared for this ordeal.

Prem *stands. The* **Women** *sit.*

Fat Auntie He eats with his mouth wide open!

Mother-in-law And sleeps with it open too, his snores rattle the windows! His poor bride will get no peace!

The **Women** *giggle and nudge each other.*

Fat Auntie But then look at the size of his big fat nose!

2nd Fat Auntie You know what they say. Big nose, big sou sou.

The **Women** *laugh.*

Mother-in-law No, that's not right! Don't you remember when we would dry him after his bath? His sou sou was so small, what did we need to find it? A magnifying glass!

Fat Auntie And have you heard that there is more hair on his hands than on his chest?

Bibi He will be bald by the time he's thirty. Look, his hair's falling out.

Prem Where? (*He looks at his shoulder.*)

Bibi It's all the whisky he drinks!

Mother-in-law That's why his eyes are pink like a rat's.

Prem I'm not here to be insulted.

Bibi That's exactly what you are here for, cretin.

Prem *fingers his nose.*

Sita Oh Prem, I thought you liked the traditions. It's traditional to respond with good humour.

Prem It's stupid!

Bibi He can't think of anything to say.

Fat Auntie He is dull witted!

Mother-in-law He was nine years of age before he could tie his shoelaces!

Prem I was eight!

The **Women** *laugh.*

Fat Auntie Is that the best you can do?

Mother-in-law Is it true he has no savings?

Fat Auntie Oh yes, it is true!

A loud whisper.

That's why he is marrying this girl.

2nd Fat Auntie (*loud whisper*) I hear she brings a cash dowry with her.

Sita (*quietly*) The insults are only for Prem. She is not here to be insulted.

Fat Auntie It is no insult to have a good dowry. It shows she comes from a provident family.

Prem Have you finished?

Fat Auntie No we have not! Come on, you young women, you are leaving us to think up insults. It is the only chance you ever get so don't waste it.

Bibi I can think of a few good ones, but Prem looks as if he's going to cry, so I won't. And look, she's crying. I don't blame her. I would if I had to marry him.

Prem You wait Bibi.

Mother-in-law Good Bibi, carry on.

Bibi If I carried on speaking the truth about Prem, this girl would get up and run from the room. So I will keep silent.

*The **Bride** wipes her eyes with the corner of her veil. **Sita** comforts her.*

Mother-in-law Sita, don't give her comfort. You will have kitchen trouble if you are too friendly.

Sita I'm not going to make an enemy of a seventeen year-old girl who is leaving her family to live amongst strangers.

Fat Auntie Prem is not a stranger. She has met him four times!

Prem They always are the night before.

Sita (*to **Indira**, the **Bride***) Do you want to marry my son?

*Shock from everyone except **Bibi**.*

Look at him!

Indira *glances briefly at **Prem** then looks away.*

Indira It is all arranged.

Sita It can all be disarranged.

Mother-in-law No it cannot! The food is ordered! The hall is booked!

Fat Auntie People are coming from the M6 and the M1!

2nd Fat Auntie She will be disgraced if the wedding is called off. Then she will never marry.

Bibi There's love marriage. Lots of the girls at school had them.

Mother-in-law A love marriage is a step into darkness hoping that you will not fall too far. But Indira's and Prem's marriage has been gone into carefully, they are well matched.

Bibi I think they are very badly matched. Indira is a nice girl but Prem is a lying sneaky bastard.

Mother-in-law That's enough Bibi.

Prem I've had enough of this. Can I go?

Mother-in-law Yes. Go.

Prem *leaves the room without a backward glance.*

Fat Auntie Come on now! Come on, start the music up, Bibi. You know how to work that machine.

Scene Two

Rose's *living-room. Loud reggae music playing.*

Rose (*off*) Delroy! Delroy! Turn that bleddy music down! *Delroy*!!! I've gorra customer with me!

Sorry to keep you waiting – I'll be out in a bit – I'm just putting me face on. Ooh, it's like plastering a wall – Max Factor oughta present me with a long service medal.

Rose *rushes on.*

Right, this is me spring catalogue. We'll have a good look through it in a bit. But I can recommend it. If it weren't for this, me and Delroy'd be going round naked. I mean, who can afford to pay cash for new stuff nowadays? I never thought I'd gerrit going. When I seen the Indians moving in round here I thought, oh well, you can say goodbye to building yourself a round up, Rose. I were a bit suspicious of 'em at first. Well, when they first come, some of 'em looked at me like I were muck. I know I ain't much, but I ain't muck. You can get used to owt can't you? And some of them are really nice – not all, but some. Any road up, as it turned out, I've got myself a nice little round going in our street. I take me catalogue round of a Wednesday, collect the money, and after we've had a few drinks, I ask 'em if they want owt else. Sita's paying me one-fifty a week for some sheets she had last year. When she's finished paying, she's having a ottoman to put 'em in.

Bibi had her first pair of jeans from out my club – Christ, didn't that cause a stink! You'd have thought she'd had a G-string or sommat! Them two old bags, bleddy Dadima an' Masi wanted Sita to send 'em back, but Sita stuck to her guns.

O'course, that were a few year ago – she's having a bit of a wobbler now. I don't know what's up, but sommat is. She's not the same girl as come here eight year ago. To tell the truth, I don't know her now. She works too hard. She's out the house at eight, and don't get back till after six, and I know she don't sit down when she gets home. She's always up and doing – has to be busy. Now I've learnt the secret of relaxation? I take life gradual, have a few laughs. It's laughing's kept me going. An it's free, so I can recommend that and all! Anyway, what you going to have?

Scene Three

The next day.

Sita *alone looking in a blank mirror touching her body.*

Sita Sita, where are you? I don't know where you are. Come back to me. You've been away so long I'm afraid that I won't know you when you come back.

Raj *enters unnoticed. He watches* **Sita** *anxiously.*

Is this you? (*She pinches her arm.*) Is this your hair? (*She pulls her hair.*) Your belly? (*She punches her own belly. Shouts.*) No it is not you! (*She beats herself. Despairing.*) Sita! Sita! I want you, please come back!

Raj, *frightened and furious, walks up to* **Sita**, *turns her in front of the mirror, forces her head until she is staring into the mirror.*

Raj You are there you mad woman, you are there. You want proof?

He slaps her and knocks her to the floor.

If you feel pain then you are there. Now get to your feet. We have visitors soon.

Raj *exits.*

Sita *gets up calmly and tidies herself, applies lipstick in the mirror, turns to leave, goes back to the mirror.*

She exits.

Scene Four

Fat Auntie, Mother-in-law *and* **Raj** *in the living-room. The same day.* **Prem** *enters smoking. He puts his cigarette in the corner of* **Fat Auntie**'s *mouth while she sleeps.*

Prem Dead good impression *she's* going to make, look at her.

Looking at **Fat Auntie.**

Mother-in-law (*to* **Fat Auntie**) Don't go to sleep now! Take that out of your mouth. They will be here soon. Look alert.

Prem How long they gonna be, Dad? I can't hang about, I've got a meet set up. There's a guy after the Datsun.

Raj If they don't come soon I'll ring and tell them to cancel. They are wasting my time.

He gets up and paces around the room.

Prem I should get three hundred quid, if he don't notice the filler.

Raj (*angry*) Two more minutes then I ring.

Prem Is this the one whose dad's got the video shops?

Raj Yes, four.

Mother-in-law Hear that sister? Video shops. We'll be all right for films, eh?

Fat Auntie Let's hope she accepts this time.

Prem She reckons she don't want to get married.

Mother-in-law She is twenty years old, time is passing. People will be thinking there is something wrong with her.

The bell rings.

Raj (*shouting*) Sita! They're here.

Sita (*off*) I know, I'm going.

Mother-in-law Everybody sit up! Look respectable.

Raj *goes to the door as two men enter. One is* **Mr Patel** *the other is his son* **Ram** *who is wearing flared trousers.*

Mr Patel (*shaking hands with* **Raj**) I am most sorry to be so late.

Ram *looks shy, awkward.*

Raj Not at all, not at all, are you late? I didn't notice. This way. My mother, my aunt and my son.

Prem (*giving his card to* **Mr Patel**) My card – Prakesh Motors.

Mr Patel Thank you. So you are in the car business?

Prem Purveyor of quality secondhand vehicles.

Mother-in-law Excuse me. I have kitchen work to do.

Mother-in-law *stares at* **Ram Patel** *before she leaves the room.*

Raj Please sit down.

They all sit. Long pause.

So how old is your son?

Mr Patel Twenty-one years.

Prem How many 'A' levels has he got?

Mr Patel Ram, show these people that you have a tongue.

Ram (*shy*) No 'A' levels, but three 'O' levels, English, maths and physics.

Mr Patel Good grades, nothing below a B.

Fat Auntie And have you had rickets?

Ram No.

An awkward silence.

Mr Patel He has passed his driving test.

Fat Auntie First time?

Mr Patel No third.

Prem Passed mine first time.

Fat Auntie What is his character like? I can see that he is shy.

Mr Patel Yes, he is a shy extrovert.

Fat Auntie What is that, extrovert?

Raj Always laughing.

Fat Auntie Heh! This one?

Mr Patel Speak up Ram. Talk about your hobbies.

Ram I like films and television and I write poetry.

Prem Poetry!?

Ram It is no good but . . .

Mr Patel Of course it is good. It is excellent poetry.

Fat Auntie And what are his vices?

Mr Patel He hasn't got any vices have you, Ram?

Ram I eat sweets. And my room is untidy sometimes.

Mr Patel The first is nothing. The second a wife will correct.

An awkward pause.

Raj Ah, the women with the food.

The Women enter carrying tit-bits of food.

My mother you've met, my wife. My daughter Bibi. Beautiful, isn't she?

Ram Hello.

Bibi Hello.

Mr Patel Bibi is how old?

Raj Eighteen.

Bibi (*corrects*) Twenty. I've got three 'A' levels.

Everyone takes a piece of food.

Raj Bibi cooked this herself, didn't you Bibi?

Bibi No Ma cooked it. I don't like cooking.

Mother-in-law (*alarm*) She likes to joke! She is a slave to the stove. We have to tear her away.

Mr Patel A sense of humour is a good thing – in moderation.

Raj Bibi is moderate in most things, aren't you Bibi?

Bibi No, I am considered extreme in most things.

Raj Again she jokes, she is so happy and cheerful!

Fat Auntie Stand up and show yourself girl.

Bibi *stands, does a twirl.*

Bibi I am twenty years old, Hindu. I am five feet six inches tall. My complexion is good, my skin tone light, my teeth (*She bares her gums.*) are perfect. I have two fillings, gold. I weigh nine stone when I am naked. My shoe size is five and a half, my pelvis is wide. Naturally I will have many sons. I speak English, Hindi, Gujerati, a little Punjabi, and French. I read two library books a week. I cook good

chappatis and can make my own clothes. I have a light melodious
singing voice, I dance gracefully and I am currently working in the
gas offices where I earn £95 a week before tax.

She sits down to silence. A pause. She rises again.

And most important of all. I am a virgin.

Prem (*under his breath*) Fucking hell.

She sits down to horrified silence. She rises again.

Bibi Sorry. My dowry consists of blankets, sheets, an electric
toaster, a fridge freezer, a portable colour television . . . a magi-mix
with full accessories.

Mr Patel Come, Ram. The girl is laughing at us.

Mother-in-law She must be ill. She has never spoken like this
before. Call for a doctor.

Sita She's not ill. She told the truth!

Raj Sita! (**Sita** *and* **Bibi** *stand together.*)

Sita She told them what they came to find out. Why waste
everyone's time with fine words?

Mr Patel She is too Western. We want a traditional girl.

Mr Patel *and* **Ram** *back out of the room.*

Sita Go on then, go and look for your kitchen slave. My daughter
will be an executive one day. She will have her own mortgage. She
has money saved in the Leicester Building Society!

The **Patels** *exit.*

Mother-in-law Why doesn't she stick a knife in my heart and be
done with it? (*To* **Sita**.) Go on, kill me now!

Fat Auntie It's her fault Bibi is so outspoken.

Raj (*to* **Bibi**) By tonight the whole of the community will have
learnt of our shame.

Bibi Stop bringing them to the house, Pa.

Prem Four video shops and she blew it.

Bibi You think I'd marry a man wearing flared trousers?

Prem (*shouting*) For four fucking video shops *I'd* marry a man in
flared trousers.

Sita She's going to buy land and a cow!

Bibi Ma I've only got thirty pounds saved.

Bibi *goes to leave the room.*

Raj Where are you going?

Bibi Out!

Bibi *exits.* **Raj** *sits with his head in his hands.*

From now on the rest of the family treat **Sita** *as though she were invisible.*

Mother-in-law Your wife is sick in the head. Cows! And land!

Fat Auntie Did you notice the strange look in her eye lately? I did.

Sita Who are you talking about? What strange look?

Mother-in-law Pressure takes different women different ways.

Raj But she's had no pressure.

Prem What about at work? She's a supervisor.

Sita You're talking about me?

Raj I should have stopped her years ago! I blame myself.

Sita Raj, I'm here look.

Mother-in-law You've got a soft heart, son. Sometimes it can be a curse.

Sita I'm here!

Fat Auntie It stops you doing your duty.

Sita Auntie!

Prem It's not as if she needs to work is it? Not now there's three of us bringing money home?

Sita Prem, can you see me?

Mother-in-law Yes, you must stop her working, Raj. Make her take a rest. We'll look after her won't we, sister?

Fat Auntie Yes. We'll take her to the doctor's.

Raj No, I'll take her. I'll make an appointment.

Sita I'm not sick!

Prem I reckon she started cracking up about the time of my wedding.

Mother-in-law The wedding that never was, poor boy.

Sita Ma Ge.

Prem It was all her fault it was called off.

Sita The girl didn't like you, she was brave enough to say no.

Mother-in-law People don't want madness in the family, who can blame them?

Sita (*shouting*) I'm standing here in front of you!

Fat Auntie Where is she?

Mother-in-law She'll be mooning over that stupid old bucket.

Fat Auntie You see? Only a mad person would do such a thing.

Raj I'll go and see.

Raj *crosses right in front of* **Sita** *and exits.*

Scene Five

The loo in the Palais. Midnight.

Bibi Well, I had a brilliant time tonight. Debauchery galore there was. I've been with every bloke in the Palais – must be 200. I came in at eight and it's Cinderella time now. So it's not bad going is it? It's my legs you see. One glimpse and the English blokes are sitting on their haunches panting for it and I'm so depraved and corrupted by the West that I let them have it. You see I've no morality of my own. No respect for my body. I've got three 'A' levels but no intelligence. I can't be trusted, after all I'm only twenty. Mum knows I come here. There's nothing I wouldn't tell her – well the odd thing. But Mum doesn't count for much in our family. When it's not at Sketchleys I keep me gear in a black plastic bag in Mum's wardrobe, next to her bucket. It's pathetic. Here I am an Asian girl caught in a culture clash. See these things each side of my head? Inverted commas. Now the English *are* lucky – they don't have family problems. No, they sit around in shafts of sunlight eating cornflakes, then get up and run around meadows in slow motion. One in four that is. The other three are undergoing divorce or family therapy. Yes we all jostle for space on the *Guardian* Women's Page. There's me, cheek by jowl with 'Shall I, a committed Socialist, send my Rupert to public school?' Now that *would* make you toss and turn at night. I'm educated. I'm healthy, and I'll make myself some sort of life. But until then I'll change in the bog. Me mum's got enough on her plate. (*Pause.*) If anyone asks, I've been babysitting.

Scene Six

Dr Mistry's *surgery. The next day.* **Raj** *and* **Sita,** *seated.* **Dr Mistry** *pacing about.*

Dr Mistry So there are no problems in your family?

Raj No, no problems. My son is in business now, my daughter passed her 'As' and will marry soon. We have a comfortable home. No, no problems.

Dr Mistry Your wife is obsessed with cows you say?

Raj Obsessed?

Dr Mistry A medical term. It means morbidly interested.

Raj Yes, she is morbidly interested in cows.

Sita There is only one cow.

Dr Mistry Yes, naturally Mrs Prakesh. Of course there is only one cow.

Sita Her name is Princess.

Raj You see?

Dr Mistry Charming. She is a pretty cow?

Sita Not particularly. Her eyes are nice but she was really nothing special. She wasn't a film star.

Dr Mistry No, naturally.

Raj What will become of her? (*He weeps.*)

Dr Mistry I see many women like her.

Raj All morbidly interested in cows?

Dr Mistry No, your wife is lucky, at least this cow seems to give her pleasure. (*To* **Sita**.) You like this cow don't you Mrs Prakesh?

Sita She is everything to me.

Raj Perhaps if she'd had more children. It is my fault! I will never forgive myself.

Dr Mistry You have had your testicles tied?

Raj No, but I failed to impregnate her more than twice. Even her womb is stubborn.

Sita *laughs.*

Dr Mistry I will give you a prescription. You must make sure your wife takes the tablets I prescribe.

Raj Will she stop thinking about the cow?

Dr Mistry Oh yes. She will stop thinking altogether. Good morning.

Dr Mistry *stands.* **Raj** *and* **Sita** *exit.*

Scene Seven

Two months later.

Sita *is sitting in the ward of a mental hospital. She is perfectly composed, thinking.*

Nurse Visitors, Mrs Prakesh. (*Pause.*) Mrs Prakesh!

She shakes **Sita** *gently.*

Sita I want to go home. I'm not mad.

Nurse No, you are just here for a rest, aren't you?

Sita Not even that, I was not tired.

Raj, Bibi, Prem, Mother-in-law, Fat Auntie *enter.* **Bibi** *runs up to* **Sita** *and holds her tight.*

Mother-in-law To see her in such a place! I can't bear it, it will kill me. All these crazy people we passed.

Fat Auntie Did you do the right thing, Raj? She is looking perfectly calm now.

Raj I listened to the doctor's advice. I am not an expert in these affairs.

Bibi But you know your own wife.

Prem She was round the bend. You know she was. Cows! Cows! Cows!

Sita (*to* **Raj**) You put me in here. (*To* **Prem**.) And you.

Fat Auntie *and* **Mother-in-law** *fuss with the food looking for somewhere to put it.*

Prem Don't blame me!

Raj You were behaving so strangely, Sita.

Fat Auntie We have brought food for you, Sita. You must eat it all up and get well again.

Mother-in-law Will Raj put *me* in this place if I lose my keys again?

Fat Auntie No. Of course not. I won't let him.(*Pause.*) And what about me? I have been having strange thoughts lately.

Mother-in-law Thoughts?

Fat Auntie Yes. About so many things. Wrong things. Things I can't say aloud.

Mother-in-law Then don't say them aloud.

Fat Auntie But I can't stop my brain from thinking, sister.

Mother-in-law We are too old to start thinking.

Sita Bibi, the next time you come bring my bucket, will you?

Prem The hospital won't allow it, Mama.

Raj There are bound to be regulations, rules.

Bibi Yes, Mama I'll bring the bucket.

Mother-in-law Lila was asking for you, Sita. She sends her love and says work is now a dull place without you.

Raj Dull without Sita?

Mother-in-law Sita was the life and soul. That's what Lila said, the life and soul. I don't know what it means.

Prem It means Mama was good for a laugh, that can't be right.

Raj No, that *can't* be right.

Bibi That's what you think. We have a really good time don't we, Ma?

Sita When they let us.

Fat Auntie (*to* **Mother-in-law**) That is what I have been thinking! I have needed permission all my life. Permission. Father, husband, Raj, and if I live long enough, Prem. Permission, always permission.

Mother-in-law Sister keep your thoughts to yourself! You have stored them away in a jar like a good housewife for 40 years. Don't let them out to spoil in the air.

Bibi Masi, we'll sit up and talk tonight. And you Dadima don't go to bed at nine. Let's stay up late and keep each other company, eh?

Mother-in-law What will we talk about for so long?

Bibi We will open Auntie's jar and see what is inside eh?

Prem If you ask me you all belong in the loony bin.

Mother-in-law Nobody is asking you are they. So shut your ugly mouth.

Shock.

Oh I'm sorry, it is this place. It made me forget myself.

Prem *looks at his watch.*

Prem I've got to be somewhere in half an hour so when you're ready . . .

Mother-in-law Oh, we'd better go.

Bibi No, we've only just arrived.

Raj But Prem is driving so . . .

Bibi So I will phone for a taxi. We can be independent of Prem to get around

Fat Auntie Yes, I never thought of a taxi. Simple isn't it?

Sita Don't look so unhappy, Prem. Go and keep your appointment. I can see that you don't like to be here. Take your father with you.

Raj But I'm not ready to go yet.

Prem Are you coming or do you wanna go home with the women?

Raj *and* **Prem** *exit.*

Scene Eight

The living-room. Later that day.

Prem *is sitting with the Princess photograph in his hand.* **Bibi** *enters. She hesitates before moving toward* **Prem**. **Prem** *doesn't notice* **Bibi** *until she pulls the photograph out of his hand.* **Bibi** *looks at the photo.*

Bibi I thought it was lost. I haven't seen it for years. God, I was skinny then!

Prem I had it in my wallet. I donno why I hated that cow.

Pause.

It just about cracked me up seeing her in there.

Bibi You were quick enough to take her in!

Prem I only drove the car. I didn't sign the papers! She hates me.

Bibi No, but she doesn't like what you've become and neither do I.

Prem The others like me.

Bibi You're their insurance policy, Prem. You'll be head of the house one day, you thick git!

Prem I didn't ask to be head of the house. I don't want them all on my back. I wanna live my own life.

Bibi Well, you've got a few years yet.

Prem What's gonna happen to Ma?

Bibi That's up to you.

Prem And you.

Bibi Since when did I have any influence over anything?

Prem Well I'm not doing it on me own. When I were driving back I kept thinking about in India. I donno how she did it. Bringing us up on us own. No money, just that cowin' cow.

Bibi She did it 'cos she's a bleddy wonderful woman.

Prem (*pause*) We should have stayed in India.

Bibi D'you reckon? I'm glad we came, I wouldn't have got three 'A' levels at the village school would I?

Prem You couldn't call it a school. It were a patch of ground under a tree.

Bibi And look how well you're doing with your garage.

Prem It's only a lock-up under a railway arch.

Bibi It's a start. You'd be a rich man in India.

Prem I wouldn't mind going back. Just to see it like.

Bibi Yeah.

Prem I'll go and see Ma tomorrow, on me own.

Bibi Take her the photo, she'd like that.

Prem No, I want the photo.

Scene Nine

One month later.

Sita *sitting in the mental hospital ward, her bucket at her feet. A* **Patient** *enters and stands to one side.* **Kishwar** *enters wearing a borqa.*

Sita Kishwar, is that you?

Kishwar Sita! Is that your voice?

Sita Yes, it's me. (*She takes* **Kishwar**'*s hands.*) Why are you here?

Kishwar I have lost my face. Why are you here?

Sita I want to buy a cow.

Kishwar Have you seen my face, Sita?

Sita No I have never seen your face. When did you see it last?

Kishwar I'm sure I had it last year. Perhaps I left it somewhere.

Sita Somewhere in the house?

Kishwar Yes, I have not left the house until this day so it is somewhere in the house. I have asked everyone. Have you seen my face? Where is my face? They say, Kishwar your face is still there. But it's not. It's not. It's gone.

Sita Let me see for myself.

Kishwar No.

Sita *raises* **Kishwar**'*s veil. There is nothing there.*

Sita You have not lost your face, Kishwar. It has been stolen.

The **Patient** *and* **Sita** *comfort* **Kishwar**.

Scene Ten

Mother-in-law, **Fat Auntie**, **Bibi** and **Lila** *enter. The* **Patient** *exits.*

Lila Sita!

She runs to **Sita**.

Sita Lila!

Lila They told me you were crazy! But look at you, you were pretending, eh? To get a rest!

Sita You're the one who should be in here. You were always a madwoman.

Lila When they told me you had gone crazy on cows, I said so what? If she wants a cow, buy her a cow.

Mother-in-law How are you Daughter?

Sita I am well. But I want to leave here now. This is a very sad place you know. It is depressing me.

Bibi I talked to the doctor.

Sita Him? He's mad. Don't listen to anything he says.

Bibi He says that you can come out for the day.

Sita Out? Do you mean home?

Bibi Yes, if you want to . . .

Lila Home! She doesn't want to go to boring home. I have the car. We will go out for a run. See the countryside.

Fat Auntie Oh yes! I mean whatever everyone else would like to do. Sita? It's your day.

Sita I can choose? What a gift!

Bibi Do you want to go to the country?

Sita Yes, could we walk on the grass?

Bibi You can take your clothes off and roll in the grass if you want to.

Mother-in-law No, that is going too far.

Fat Auntie But we have no food!

Lila There are cafés, shops, this is Leicestershire, not the foothills of the Himalayas. Well, what are we waiting for?

Bibi Come on, Ma.

Mother-in-law An adventure. (*She clasps her hands girlishly.*) Where are we going?

Lila Who knows? I will get behind the wheel and let the car take us where it wants.

Scene Eleven

The **Women**, *travelling in the car.*

Fat Auntie Not so fast Lila!

Lila I have slowed down to 30. Nice country, eh.

Mother-in-law I don't know, my eyes are shut.

Bibi Isn't it lovely Lila? It was near here I came camping with the Guides. My first night away from home. I cried so much Akala brought me home the next day.

Fat Auntie And you taught us all that terrible song about goolies.

Mother-in-law With words for idiots.

Sita I thought it was a foreign language, French. I thought it was French.

Sita *sings 'Ging gang gooly'. Everyone joins in.*

Look cows! Stop the car!

Groans from everyone else but **Bibi**.

Bibi Stop the car, Lila. Stop!

Lila *stops the car.*

Mother-in-law Remember the green cross code!

Sita *crosses the road. She runs to the fence, looks into the meadow. Two* **Cows** *approach the fence.*

Sita Hello. How are you?

Both Cows Not happy. We are going to the market today.

Sita Do you know Princess?

1st Cow Princess?

2nd Cow From India?

Sita Yes, that's her.

1st Cow Mummm.

Sita She is looking for me. Will you tell her where I am?

Both Cows Mummm.

Sita Where is the market?

2nd Cow Melton Mowbray, just down the road.

Sita Thank you, goodbye. (**Sita** *crosses the road and gets into the car.*)

Both Cows Morning.

1st Cow ⎫ Nice woman.
2nd Cow ⎭ Good smell.

Sita We are going to Melton Mowbray.

Lila Where is that?

Sita That cow said it was just down the road.

Mother-in-law Ay ay ay.

Fat Auntie A cow told you? How can you believe a cow? In my experience they are very unreliable. You have heard the expression, 'lying cow'?

Mother-in-law Yes. Better look at the map.

Scene Twelve

The cattle market.

The **Women** *enter the showing area. They look at the ring. An* **Auctioneer** *and a stockman,* **Harold**, *are talking at the side entrance gate.*

Mother-in-law Chi, what a stink! My nose thinks it has been dipped in a sewer.

Auctioneer Now there's a nice one for my collection.

Harold Never had a brown 'un?

Auctioneer Never had the opportunity, Harold. Don't see many Asiatics round here.

Fat Auntie Watch where you're putting your feet, Sita. You're getting cow dung on your sandals.

Harold Look at the arse on that one. (*He goes to whistle at* **Bibi** *but the* **Auctioneer** *stops him.*)

Auctioneer Not so crude, Harold, they're easily frightened.

Lila You belong in a straight jacket, Sita. A day out and you choose to trample in cow shit!

The **Women** *laugh.*

Auctioneer (*to the* **Women**) Morning ladies. (*He tips his hat slightly.*)

Women Morning. (*They are quite pleased at this politeness.*)

Auctioneer Can we be of any assistance?

Bibi No thank you, we're going now. Have you seen enough, Ma?

Sita Yes. I don't like it here. I want to go.

Harold This is a short cut ladies.

He opens the gate. The **Women** *walk towards the gate and are about to pass by the* **Men** *when* **Harold** *grabs* **Bibi**'s *wrist.*

Women Thank you.

Harold Nearly fell din't you?

Bibi No I didn't, let go! (**Harold** *continues holding* **Bibi**'s *wrist.*)

Auctioneer While you're here, I'd just like to say that you've got the nicest pair of tits I've seen in a lifetime's study.

Bibi, *shocked, instinctively covers her breasts with her free hand.*

Lila You dirty bastard!

Auctioneer Foul mouthed cow!

Sita *is chopping at* **Harold**'s *hand holding* **Bibi**'s *wrist.*

Sita Let my daughter go! (**Harold** *fondles* **Bibi**'s *bum.*)

Bibi Mama!

Auctioneer Shut the other gate, Harold. We'll have a good look at 'em.

Harold *closes the back gate, trapping the* **Women**. *The* **Auctioneer** *closes the side gate.* **Lila** *rushes to the side gate, tries to open it.*

Auctioneer Give her a bit of stick, Harold!

Harold *hits* **Lila** *hard. She runs around the ring as a cow.*

Harold Gwaan gwaan, move round you stubborn buggers!

The **Auctioneer** *stands on his podium.*

Auctioneer Get 'em moving, Harold!

Harold *pokes the stick into the group of women. The* **Women** *move apart a little and run round the ring.*

Auctioneer Separate them out, Harold. Get 'em running. Go on Harold show 'em who's master.

Mr Patel *enters. He stands at the side of the ring appraising the* **Women**.

Harold Geed up! Geed up! Go on run you buggers!

Auctioneer A small herd and a rarity in these parts. Pedigree Indian stock. Good breeders and three guaranteed milkers. What am I bid for a herd? C'mon gentlemen, what am I bid? No bids? C'mon gentlemen, who'll start? Who'll start? No bids? Get rid of the old uns, Harold.

Harold *forces* **Mother-in-law** *and* **Fat Auntie** *to the side of the ring. They stand together. The other three* **Women** *continue round the ring.*

Auctioneer Three milkers gentlemen, fine colour, a rarity. What am I bid?

This is repeated five times. **Mr Patel** *shakes his head slightly.*

No takers. Show us the young un, Harold.

Harold *forces* **Sita** *and* **Lila** *to the side of the ring. The* **Women** *herd together. They make low distressed cow noises.* **Bibi** *moves slowly making whimpering cow noises.* **Mr Patel** *takes part in the bidding.*

Auctioneer A youngun. A youngun. Full udders. Fine legs. Good colour. A hundred and fifteen! And twenty! Twenty-five, thirty, thirty-five, *two hundred, two hundred.*Two hundred and fifty-and seventy. Eighty. Three, Three, Three-Three hundred and two, five and fifty. Seven five. Four hundred . . . and fifty. Five. Five hundred. Six hundred. That's more like it. Seven. Eight. A thousand. Two hundred and three. Three, four, five a thousand five hundred! Five hundred. Six, seven, eight. Two thousand five hundred. Sold to Mr Patel! Take her away Harold.

Harold *prods* **Bibi**.

Harold Move you cow!

Bibi *straightens up then tries to run away. But* **Harold** *pushes her down, pins her to the ground and forces her legs apart.* **Bibi** *screams.*

Sita *leads the other* **Women** *into Kali sequence. They bear down on* **Harold**.

Auctioneer Settle 'em down, Harold! They're getting out of control.

Bibi *joins the* **Women**.

Use your stick, man!

The **Women** *continue moving in on* **Harold**.

The **Auctioneer** *runs from his podium and through the gate, leaving it open. The* **Women** *continue towards* **Harold**. *He threatens them with his stick.*

The **Auctioneer** *runs into the ring.*

Now get back! Move back! I'm used to being obeyed!

The **Auctioneer** *is knocked out of the way. He runs out of the ring.*

Harold *raises his stick to attack the* **Women** *but* **Sita** *pulls it from him.* **Harold** *falls on the floor.* **Sita** *stands over him threatening him with the stick.*

Harold Don't kill me, please! Please! Please! I'm sorry.

The **Women** *begin to normalise.* **Harold** *takes a chance and jumps up.*

You want locking up! You're fucking mad the whole lot of you.

Auctioneer If you're not out of here in one minute I'm phoning the police.

The **Auctioneer** *and* **Harold** *go.*

Sita Call the police, we'll do the same to them!

The **Women** *jeer and gesticulate at the* **Men**. **Mother-in-law** *makes particularly violent gestures.*

Lila I'll fetch the car round. (*As she exits.*) Don't let Dadima out of your sight eh? She's not safe.

The **Women** *laugh and tidy themselves.*

Sita Are you hurt, Bibi?

Bibi I don't know. I'm too high to care.

Fat Auntie My legs are wobbling. So much exercise!

Mother-in-law But we got rid of the demons didn't we? How they ran!

Bibi They were only men Mam, hardly demons.

Sita Anyone that treats my daughter in that way is a demon. And will get the same treatment.

They start to go.

Fat Auntie Listen to her.

Mother-in-law They got what they deserved.

Scene Thirteen

The mental hospital.

Sita *and* **Bibi** *enter the ward singing a snatch of 'Ging gang gooly'.*

Bibi (*half laughing*) Don't tell 'em what happened or they will have you in a straight jacket.

Sita I'll say we had a quiet picnic.

Bibi Some picnic!

They laugh. The **Nurse** *enters carrying tea.*

Nurse You're tea, no sugar, aren't you Mrs Prakash?

Sita Yes. (*Pause. She takes the tea.*) Have you put anything in it?

Nurse (*laughing*) So suspicious! (*She looks at* **Sita**.) You're looking well. The fresh air did you good.

Sita Yes, we're leaving soon.

Nurse Oh you are, are you? Where are you going?

The **Nurse** *looks at* **Sita** *and* **Bibi**. **Bibi** *shrugs.*

The **Nurse** *hands* **Sita** *a small pill cup and stands, expecting* **Sita** *to swallow the pill inside.*

Nurse (*kindly*) It's a lower dosage.

Bibi Go on, Ma. You'll be off them soon.

Nurse Yes I'll have a word with the doctor tomorrow.

Sita *pretends to swallow the pill. She does this skilfully, the audience shouldn't notice.*

You're doing very well.

Sita I know.

The **Nurse** *exits.*

Good she's gone. Now we can go to India.

Bibi India! When were you thinking of going?

Sita Tonight.

Bibi I can't come tonight, Ma. In fact I don't want to go at all. I've got my work you see.

Sita Then you must come for a long visit. You and Prem.

Bibi Oh yes. I'd love a holiday there.

Sita I'll be off as soon as I find Princess. She's very near now. Are you sure you'll be all right in England?

Bibi Of course I will. I like it. It's where I live.

Sita Good. Then I needn't worry about you?

Bibi I'll come and see you tomorrow. Do you want me to bring anything in?

Sita But I won't be here. I'll be in India. Goodbye, my darling girl. Give my love to the family. Oh and Bibi, get rid of this.

She hands **Bibi** *the pill.*

Bibi Yes I will. Sleep well.

Bibi *exits.*

Sita Come on Princess, I know you're there.

That's it Princess, this way, look I'm here.

Princess *appears in the window.*

How beautiful you look, not a day older. I've been waiting for you for so long, but now I can go home.

She puts her hand on the window.

Scene Fourteen

The Indian village, early morning as in Act One, Scene One.

Sita *is milking and watching* **Bibi** *and* **Prem** *who are playing a game with a small stick and a block of wood. They are happy.* ·

Mother-in-law *and* **Fat Auntie** *are mending the photographer's bicycle.*

Mother-in-law We got a bargain eh, sister?

Fat Auntie That crazy photographer, to sell his bike for fifty rupees.

Prem When it's mended can I ride it?

Mother-in-law No, it's too big for you. You will fall off and break your head in half.

Prem But I want to ride it and I will ride it!

Fat Auntie (*sternly*) No! Carry on with your game and move out of our way!

Prem Who's it for if it's not for me?

Fat Auntie It's for Bibi.

Prem Girls don't ride bicycles.

Sita Bibi go and show that boy that he's wrong.

Bibi But I don't know how to ride it.

Fat Auntie Of course you don't know, but you'll have to learn. Now get on it.

Bibi *gets on.*

Bibi But why me?

Fat Auntie You're the eldest. You will need it for secondary school.

Mother-in-law Now we both take a side and support you. Turn the pedals, Bibi. You must do some of the work yourself.

They support **Bibi** *as she wobbles around the compound.*

Prem My sister riding a bike! I am the only boy in the village whose sister can ride a bike! Go on Bibi, do it by yourself now!

Bibi *rides alone.*

Bibi Look Ma, I can do it. I can do it!